I hope that you will take home
happy memories of England.
From a grateful patient

Thomas H. Marshall

THE FIRST COUNTRY LIFE

PICTURE BOOK OF LONDON

WESTMINSTER BRIDGE AND THE HOUSES OF PARLIAMENT, FROM LONDON'S COUNTY HALL

THE FIRST COUNTRY LIFE

PICTURE BOOK
OF LONDON

WITH AN INTRODUCTION BY

JOHN CODRINGTON

COUNTRY LIFE LIMITED LONDON

First published in 1951
by Country Life Limited
Tavistock Street London WC2
Process engraving by
The Sun Engraving Co Ltd London
Printed in Great Britain by
Balding & Mansell Ltd
London and Wisbech
Revised Edition
(*Fifth impression*) 1964

LONDON

LONDON is a name all the world knows, and every year from every country come thousands of visitors to see London.

But how many of these visitors go away with a slight sense of disappointment? London has few of the splendid wide avenues and long vistas of Paris, few of the beauties of past centuries such as crowd upon the visitor to Rome. She cannot boast the baroque of Vienna or the arresting skyline of New York, and her charm does not jump to the eye of the new arrival.

Yet London has 'something', though it is a 'something' that is not immediately obvious. The visitor has to dig for it and sense it gradually. That is why quite a number of people with somewhat superficial minds, or in too much of a hurry for quick effects, miss the point of London and are apt to be disappointed.

The pictures in this book set out to help such people to realize the soul and unexpected beauty of this great town which is a county containing two cities, twenty-seven boroughs and many suburbs besides, and which is also the largest port in the world besides being the capital of the British Empire and Commonwealth of Nations.

How did it all happen? To appreciate London properly a quick glance through its history is essential; then things that at first seemed puzzling fall into their proper places.

London began because of the River Thames. It is not a very long river, as rivers go, but it has a wide and deep estuary with a tide that rises and falls some fifteen feet and keeps the channel dredged and navigable right into the heart of the City.

The Romans, the Saxons, the Danes and the Normans all appreciated this, and the Romans built their City with its forum and temples on the heights on the north bank of the Thames. They built a wall around it, parts of which are still to be seen today, and which extended roughly in a semi-circle with a radius of about half a mile from London Bridge.

After the Romans left Britain, London lay derelict for a long time. Some of the ancient British and Celtic inhabitants began to drift back, but they could not withstand the Saxon pirates who came in from the sea and gradually settled round the Roman ruins in 'tons' or fortified villages (such as Charlton, Islington, Paddington, Kensington, Kennington) or homesteads or 'hams' (such as Clapham, Eltham, West and East Ham, Fulham, Hampstead).

The part of this great town known as the City of London to this day roughly corresponds to the area of the old Roman City of Londinium; and her twisting streets probably follow the tracks which the Saxon shepherds made with their sheep. And the great estuary up which sailed St Olaf of Norway and Cnut the Dane and all the commerce from across the North Sea is still the foundation of the importance of the City.

But meanwhile another influence of London's destiny was in the making. About a mile and a half upstream to the west from London Bridge, on a desolate island covered with thorns and brambles in the marshes, some monks founded a monastery. Already in the City of London a cathedral dedicated to St Paul was arising; the monastery on Thorney Island became the monastery or minster in the west, and today we know its successor as Westminster Abbey. The saintly king, Edward the Confessor, enriched and endowed the abbey, making his palace nearby. The church has been rebuilt several times since his day, but his body still lies in his shrine behind the High Altar of the great church of St Peter in Westminster.

The Royal connexion endured. The kings of England have lived in Westminster on and off for some nine hundred years and have all—except Edward V and Edward VIII—been crowned in the Abbey. In 1900 Westminster was given the title of 'City', and is thus the second city within the town of London. The City (of London) itself is the historic core of this great place, and the heart of its trade and commerce today as it has been all down the ages, while the City of Westminster is, and has always been, the seat of Government and the residence of the monarch and court.

Gradually the City of London became so congested that many of the wealthier inhabitants and peers of the realm built riverside houses and palaces along the strand or foreshore of the Thames upstream towards Westminster, where the court was, and so gradually the link-up between the two cities took place along what is still called The Strand.

Over against the City of London on the south bank of the river was the southern outwork or bulwark defending the approaches to London Bridge. It became the first suburb or borough outside the walls, and the borough of Southwark is still known as *the* Borough to all Londoners, and has a history almost as ancient as the parent city. It now has its own cathedral for the vast area of present-day London south of the Thames.

Gradually the little Saxon hamlets and villages became joined to the central masses of London and Westminster. In Charles I's reign the laying out of Covent Garden and Lincoln's Inn Fields under the supervision of Inigo Jones gave London its first regularly planned open spaces with houses ranged round them which are so characteristic of our metropolis. The arcaded houses of Covent Garden have been pulled down and the vegetable market now covers most of the open space, but Jones's church, St Paul's, still stands at the west end, albeit reconstructed after a fire. The Great Fire of London in 1666 necessitated the rebuilding of the greater part of the City. For half a century building activity was concentrated on this formidable task and so, while St Paul's was slowly rising and Wren's steeples were taking their places one by one on the London sky-line, the outward expansion of the metropolis was inevitably slowed down; but already before the Fire the first London squares to be so called—Bloomsbury Square and St James's Square—had begun to take shape. The characteristic London house, simple, restrained and dignified, with beautifully designed doorway and graceful ironwork, made its appearance.

For a century and a half, with but slight modifications arising from changes in taste and fashion, the typical London house continued to take its place in street and square as these multiplied in Bloomsbury and Mayfair and farther out beyond Oxford Street. The outward pressure was growing under the first two Georges, but it was immensely increased during the long reign of George III, to which most of the Georgian squares of London belong. No other capital city, Dublin and Edinburgh excepted, can parallel this remarkable achievement in town-planning, effected with typical English reticence and absence of display, and using for the most part workaday brick instead of stone or marble. The growth of London produced a need for new churches. Some, like St Martin-in-the-Fields, were rebuilt in classical dress, but many more—the graceful St Mary-le-Strand, for instance, and St George's, Hanover Square—were new creations, built in the white Portland stone which Wren had used so effectively in the City.

Early in the nineteenth century, with London ever spreading outwards, came the age of stucco, and the period of the Prince Regent and Nash to whom we owe the magnificent town-planning scheme which, beginning at Waterloo Place with the Duke of York's Column and Carlton House Terrace, culminates in Regent's Park with its terraces. Many other squares (grand, like Belgrave Square; modest like Victoria Square) and many more terraced streets came later. Meanwhile the surrounding villages were gradually absorbed into the mass and in many cases have become the boroughs of today with no green fields between them. The old village centre, with its green, its High Street, its parish church and its pubs can almost always still be identified, and the boroughs generally still keep that sturdy feeling of independence that is so characteristic of villages in the country.

So London goes on growing, each generation adding to it in its own style and its own way; some of it good—a lot of it bad. Almost always the development has been piecemeal, and the result of a sturdy individualism on the part of land-owners or speculative builders. London has never had an overall plan (Wren's plan for the City after the Great Fire was turned down).

And now London, battered almost ceaselessly during the last war, is rising again and is erecting new and, we hope, better buildings. The bombing destroyed much that was beautiful and old, but also much that was a perpetual disgrace to the largest city in the world. One may hope that the Londoners of the next generation will not need to be so critical of their forbears as we must often be.

It is chiefly the purpose of this Picture Book of London to help visitors to appreciate the many aspects of this great metropolis. We start with the splendid palace built by Sir Christopher Wren at Greenwich, the first of the many unexpected wonders for the traveller who comes up the Thames from the sea. We move past the Tower Bridge, that great portal to the City, a rare example of Victorian imagination, and a monument to the prosperity of the age: on to The Pool with its shipping from all over the world; and on to the Tower, the great fortress that has guarded the entrance to the City since William I's reign and has been fortress, palace and political prison ever since. (Certain traitors were imprisoned here in both the recent World Wars.)

From the grandeur of the Tower we pass to the humble waterside pub, to the City merchants, the brokers of Throgmorton Street, and the fish porters of Billingsgate—each of them different aspects of the great hive that is London. A few pictures show us the past of the City, while the 'Clink' takes us back to the grim prison (destroyed in the Gordon Riots of 1780) which gives its name to prisons wherever the English language is spoken. The City, with St Paul's dominating it, leads us from commerce to the Law, and to the Temple (in whose gardens two angry dukes are said to have plucked red and white roses centuries ago, and so started a useless but bloody civil war), and the Inns of Court. London is then seen as the centre of a famous university with the British Museum nearby, while onwards our Picture Book takes us upstream to Westminster and Whitehall with their Royal Palaces and Government Offices.

Next, in the West End, are London's theatres and places of amusement, and the lights of Piccadilly and Leicester Square, which, though on a modest scale compared with those of New York and many other cities, are much loved by Londoners. And these same Londoners love the country; they take great slabs of the countryside and enclose it with all its natural life into their town. Here sheep graze and blackbirds sing in the parks, swans and wild duck swim on the lakes, and the trees are not clipped.

Yet London does have its hours of pomp and ceremony, and the wide streets round the Royal Palaces are suitable for the splendid ceremonial and gay uniforms of the Household Troops. And so we pass through the quiet, once aristocratic West End on to literary Chelsea and Hampstead. Peacefulness and serenity are shown in the rest of the book, with the splendidly contrasting bulk of the Power Station at Chelsea to remind us that in West London there is the same throbbing energy and vitality as there is in the City and among the docks.

Thus we show this immense town as a panorama of many aspects. It is to be hoped that the visitor's appetite may be stimulated by these pictures and that he will explore and find many other equally entrancing and varied aspects of London for himself.

1951   JOHN CODRINGTON

LIST OF PLATES

ACKNOWLEDGEMENTS

Acknowledgements are due to the following who provided the photographs for this book:

G. F. Allen, *frontispiece, plates* 1, 6, 7, 9-17, 19, 23, 25, 30, 34, 43, 48, 52-54, 56-59, 67, 76-81, 83, 86-88
Sport and General, *plate* 4; Central Press, *plates* 37 and 46; Graphic Photo Union, *plate* 40.

All other illustrations are from *Country Life* photographs.

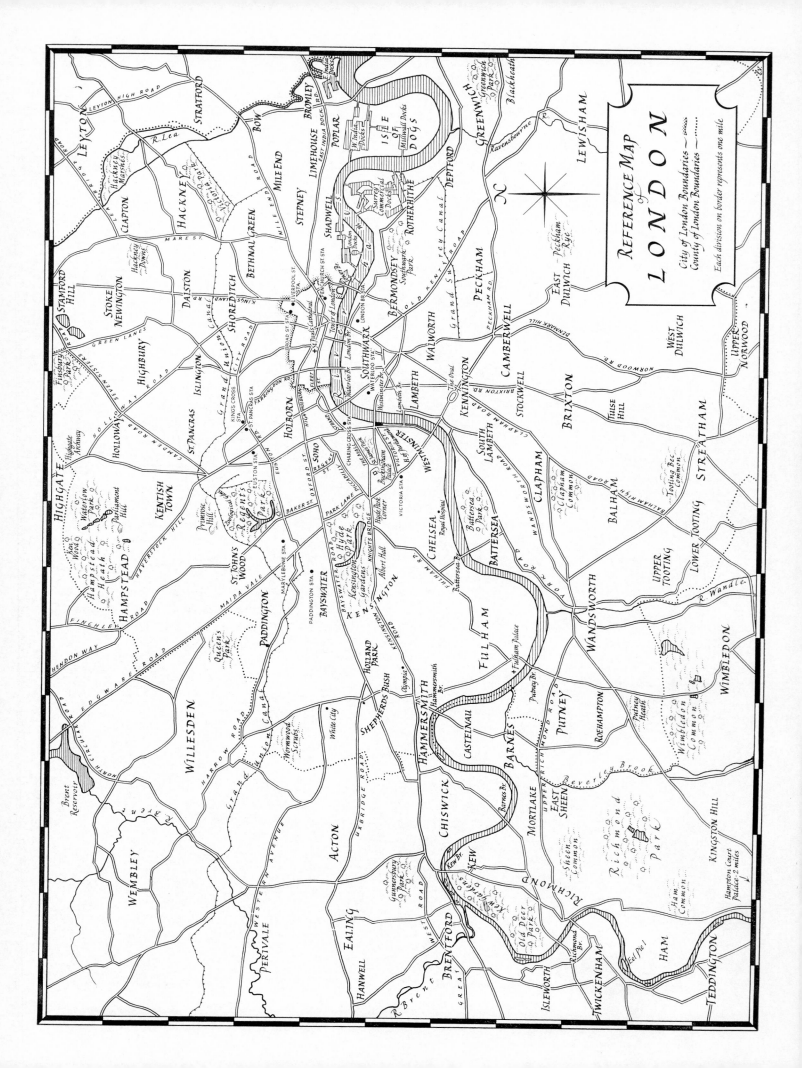

REFERENCE MAP
of
LONDON

City of London Boundaries ———
County of London Boundaries ········

Each division on border represents one mile

1. THE ROYAL HOSPITAL, GREENWICH. This noble group of Thames-side buildings, now the home of the National Maritime Museum and the Royal Naval War College, was begun by Charles II and completed to the designs of Sir Christopher Wren in the reign of William III.

2. TOWER BRIDGE, LOOKING DOWN-RIVER. Tower Bridge is the last bridge down the Thames. Beyond it lie London's great docks, and the highway to the sea. The bridge, with its raised footway 142 feet above high water, and the twin leaves of its central span, was opened in 1894.

3. THE POOL OF LONDON. A view of one of the busiest sections of the river, looking west towards London Bridge. The skyline of the north bank is dominated by the Monument, to the right of which, facing the river, is the Custom House.

4. THE YEOMAN WARDERS OF THE TOWER.   Led by the Chief Warder, the Yeoman Warders, in their scarlet uniforms and Tudor bonnets, march in procession within the precincts of the Tower that has been guarded by this famous corps for more than four hundred years.

5. THE WHITE TOWER ON TOWER HILL. The White Tower is the heart of the great fortress of the Tower of London. Built by William the Conqueror, its walls and battlements have been the settings for some of the most tragic episodes in British history.

6. 'THE PROSPECT OF WHITBY', WAPPING. This picturesque dockland inn takes its name from one of the ships out of the Yorkshire town of Whitby which, in former years, anchored here at the end of their coast-wise voyages.

7. THE MONUMENT. The two-hundred-foot column of Wren's memorial to the Great Fire of 1666 rises above streets crowded by the porters of nearby Billingsgate—for hundreds of years London's chief fish market.

8. THROGMORTON STREET. This street, which lies just behind the Bank of England, is the 'home' of London's stockbrokers. Its name recalls a Tudor statesman who was instrumental in bringing Lady Jane Grey to the throne, and was father-in-law of Sir Walter Raleigh.

9. ST MARY-LE-BOW, CHEAPSIDE. Only those born within the sound of the bells of this famous old city church are truly Londoners born. The steeple is generally considered to be the finest of those designed by Sir Christopher Wren after the Great Fire.

10. IRONMONGERS' HALL. The City of London is rich in the buildings that are the headquarters of its ancient companies. The Hall of the Ironmongers is a recent building, replacing one destroyed by a bomb in the First World War.

11. ST JOHN'S GATE, CLERKENWELL. This was once the gateway of the Priory of the Knights of St John of Jerusalem, and was built in 1504, not many years before the Order was dissolved. Now it is once more the headquarters of the Knights of the revived Order.

12. THE 'TIGER' INN, TOWER HILL. An inn of this name was standing on the site of the present building as far back as 1500, and the tradition that Queen Elizabeth visited it on her way down-river to Tilbury in 1556 is still remembered.

13. ON BANKSIDE.   Early morning, among the cranes and warehouses on the south bank of the river. Through the mist can be seen the outlines of Southwark Bridge and, beyond it, the arched roof of Cannon Street Station.

14. CLINK STREET, SOUTHWARK.   Bankside, where once stood Shakespeare's 'Globe', is now a place of tall warehouses and narrow grimy passages. Clink Street takes its name from the 'clink' or prison administered here in medieval times by the Bishops of Winchester.

15. LONDON BRIDGE AND SOUTHWARK CATHEDRAL. London Bridge as we know it was built in 1831. At its southern end stands Southwark Cathedral, famous for its associations with Shakespeare and his friends, and many other great names in English Literature.

16. THE BANK OF ENGLAND.   The Bank, in the heart of the City, was established at the end of the seventeenth century. The great new building, added to the old in this century, was designed by Sir Herbert Baker.

17. THE ROYAL EXCHANGE. The present building, opened by Queen Victoria in 1844, is the third to occupy the site since its foundation in 1571. From its steps the accession of a new sovereign is proclaimed in the City of London.

18. FLEET STREET. The view is that towards Ludgate Hill and St Paul's. Here, or nearby, are the headquarters of most of England's national newspapers and news-gathering organizations. Its name comes from the old Fleet river, now dwindled into an underground drain.

19. ST PAUL'S, FROM SOUTH BANK. The dome of St Paul's Cathedral is the noblest sight in London's skies. The Cathedral is Wren's master-work; the splendid memorial of the new London which arose from the ashes of the old after the Great Fire.

20. THE LAW COURTS. This impressive memorial of the Gothic revival of the nineteenth century was completed in 1882. It faces the Strand, just beyond 'the Griffin' which stands on a pedestal in the middle of the road and marks the beginning of Fleet Street.

21 THE STRAND. The view towards the eighteenth-century church of St Mary-le-Strand, with St Clement Danes behind it, is known all over the world, and the street itself, as much as any other in London, stands as an image of London to travellers and to exiles in distant places.

22. EXCHANGE COURT, STRAND. Many discoveries are to be made by the Londoner who turns aside from the main streets. Exchange Court, just off the Strand, is notable for its imposing eighteenth-century house, since 1859 the headquarters of the Corps of Commissionaires.

23. IN NEW SQUARE, LINCOLN'S INN, HOLBORN.   Lincoln's Inn is one of the four Inns of Court which alone have the authority to call new recruits 'to the bar'. New Square is a gracious open space enclosed by pleasant office buildings of brick.

24. MIDDLE TEMPLE LANE. This narrow passage-way, which runs between Fleet Street and the Thames Embankment, approximately divides the territories of the two great Inns of the Temple, Inner and Middle Temple.

25. MIDDLE TEMPLE HALL.   This majestic hall was opened by Queen Elizabeth in 1572. Here she danced, and here Shakespeare is believed to have acted in 'Twelfth Night' in 1602. The superbly carved oak screen and gallery are of the same age as the hall.

26. **UNIVERSITY OF LONDON, HOLBORN.** The great white tower of London's great centre of learning rises 210 feet in Bloomsbury's skies. The designer of this as yet unfinished group of buildings is Mr Charles Holden, whose work began in 1931.

27. THE BRITISH MUSEUM, HOLBORN. A corner of one of the world's greatest stores of art-treasures, which is seen by hundreds of thousands of scholars, students and visitors every year. The collection was begun in 1753 with the purchase of manuscripts assembled by Sir Hans Sloane.

28. ST PANCRAS CHURCH, EUSTON ROAD. This church, the work of William Inwood in 1820, is unique in London, and perhaps in England, for its faithful rendering of the strict Greek style. The design of the tower is based on that of the Athenian 'Tower of the Winds'.

29. IN GORDON SQUARE, BLOOMSBURY. The area of London that lies between the Euston Road and New Oxford Street is a famous centre of learning and study. It owes its charm to its many quiet squares enclosing the tree-shaded lawns and flower-beds of their gardens.

30. ON THE EMBANKMENT. 'Discovery', once commanded by Scott of the Antarctic, and veteran of many years of Polar voyages, was moored below Waterloo Bridge in 1937 as a memorial to Captain Scott and his comrades.

31. CLEOPATRA'S NEEDLE, EMBANKMENT. This famous granite column, first hewn about 1450 B.C., erected before the great temple of Heliopolis in Egypt, and then moved to Cleopatra's palace in Alexandria, was brought to this country after an adventurous sea voyage in 1878.

32. WATERLOO BRIDGE. The view from South Bank of the most modern of the great Thames bridges, designed by Sir Giles Gilbert Scott. It was opened in 1945 to replace John Rennie's old bridge—one of the most beautiful in Europe—whose foundations were discovered to be unsafe in the nineteen-twenties.

33. WESTMINSTER BRIDGE. Looking west from the Embankment to the bridge which was opened not long after the completion of the Houses of Parliament, in 1862, there is this spacious view of London's County Hall (extreme left) and the turreted blocks of St Thomas's Hospital whose history of healing goes back for more than seven hundred years.

34. HENRY VII'S CHAPEL, WESTMINSTER ABBEY. This chapel is the most glorious part of the Abbey, and its vaulted roof one of the supreme masterpieces of church architecture. It was begun in 1502, and within it are the tombs of many British Kings and Queens.

35. THE STATUE OF OLIVER CROMWELL, WESTMINSTER HALL. The splendid statue of the great Protector stands before Westminster Hall where he was proclaimed Protector. The Hall dates from 1097, in the time of William Rufus.

36. WHITEHALL.   The view of this famous street is that towards Big Ben and the Houses of Parliament. Its name stands everywhere for the government of Great Britain and the Commonwealth—for in or around it are all the great administrative offices of the State.

37. THE CENOTAPH. Her Majesty the Queen, members of the Royal Family, Cabinet ministers, and a great gathering of people in every walk of life attend the annual remembrance of the dead of two world wars at the Commonwealth's memorial in Whitehall.

38. NUMBER TEN, DOWNING STREET.   The unpretentious façade of one of the best-known houses in the world. Number Ten, the official residence of the Prime Minister, has formed part of the group of Treasury buildings since the eighteenth century.

39. KING CHARLES STREET, WHITEHALL. The view towards St James's Park through one of the arches of the bridge that connects the huge blocks of Government offices between Downing Street and Parliament Square. All have been built in the last hundred years.

40. **A STATE OPENING OF PARLIAMENT.** The royal coach turns into Whitehall from Horse Guards Parade. Behind the procession is the Horse Guards itself, an eighteenth-century building guarded by mounted sentries of the Household Cavalry.

41. WHITEHALL FROM ST JAMES'S PARK. The tower of the Foreign Office building seen across a corner of the lake of the most enchanting of London's parks. It was first emparked by Henry VIII who maintained in it a herd of deer.

42. ST JAMES'S PARK: THE LAKE. The lake (from whose central suspension bridge there is one of the loveliest views in London) stretches almost the whole length of the Park, and is the home of many rare and beautiful kinds of wildfowl.

43. WESTMINSTER CATHEDRAL. The campanile of the great Roman Catholic cathedral commands an unequalled view of Greater London. The vast building of red brick and white stone was designed by J. F. Bentley, and its first stone was laid by Cardinal Vaughan in 1895.

44. CONSTITUTION HILL, GREEN PARK. The Queen's Guard of the Royal Horse Guards rides down Constitution Hill to Whitehall. At its back is Decimus Burton's archway at the entrance to the Hill, crowned by one of the most beautiful of London's sculpture groups—Adrian Jones's 'Quadriga', erected to the memory of Edward VII.

45. DUKE OF YORK'S STEPS. At the foot of the Duke of York's column, a broad flight of steps leads into the Mall and, beyond it, to St James's Park. Facing the steps is the Royal Artillery Memorial to the dead of the South African war.

46. **LONDON'S GREAT PROCESSIONAL WAY.** The scene from Buckingham Palace as Her Majesty the Queen and the Duke of Edinburgh, with an escort of the Household Cavalry, return home from the Mall past the Victoria Memorial after their triumphant Commonwealth tour of 1953-54.

47. **THE CHANGING OF THE GUARD AT BUCKINGHAM PALACE.** Headed by the band of the Irish Guards, the new guard marches before the gates of the Palace to take up its duties. The Royal Standard flying above the Palace is a sign that the Sovereign is in residence.

48. CLARENCE HOUSE, ST JAMES'S. The view from Clarence Gate of the London home of the Queen Mother. This gracious house, facing the Mall, was rebuilt early in the nineteenth century, and was once the home of King William IV.

49. ST JAMES'S PALACE. The Tudor palace of St James's, begun for Henry VIII, is no longer the home of the sovereign; but it is still to 'Our Court of St James's' that ambassadors from foreign countries are accredited.

50. LEICESTER SQUARE. The square owes its fame to its nineteenth-century theatres (now all replaced by cinemas), and not to any elegance in its design, but the garden surrounding a statue of Shakespeare makes an attractive oasis in the heart of the West End.

51. THE HAYMARKET. This street, which is the principal traffic link between Trafalgar Square and Piccadilly Circus, is distinguished for the charming portico of the Theatre Royal, designed early in the nineteenth century by John Nash, architect of Old Regent Street.

52. TRAFALGAR SQUARE. The view of this famous square is of its eastern side: on the right the façade of South Africa House; on the left the portico and spire of St Martin-in-the-Fields, designed by James Gibbs in 1726.

53. PICCADILLY CIRCUS.   Few monuments are more widely known or better loved than Sir Alfred Gilbert's 'Eros', poised above the fountain which stands at the busy heart of London's West End. It was set up as a memorial to the great humanitarian, the Earl of Shaftesbury.

54. SHEPHERD MARKET, WESTMINSTER. This small corner of Mayfair is one of the most surprising survivals in London, for here, just off Piccadilly, the visitor finds himself among the shops and narrow streets of a small country town of the eighteenth century.

55. IN CURZON STREET, MAYFAIR. This attractive front hints at the elegance of a street which runs west to Park Lane through Mayfair, a name symbolic of London's wealth and fashion all over the world.

56. PICCADILLY, FROM HYDE PARK CORNER. Apsley House is the first of these great houses which overlook Green Park at the western end of Piccadilly. It was presented by the nation to the Duke of Wellington after the battle of Waterloo.

57. THE 'QUADRIGA': HYDE PARK CORNER. In this view of one of the busiest traffic centres in the world, the 'Quadriga' looks down on Charles Jagger's massive and sombre memorial, now dedicated to the men of the Royal Artillery who died in two world wars.

58. 93, PARK LANE. Built in 1827, this is one of the last survivors of the Regency houses of Park Lane, now known for its great modern hotels and office buildings. This was the London home of Disraeli from 1839 to 1873.

59. HYDE PARK CORNER.   The view, over Decimus Burton's graceful triple-arched entrance screen, of the Hyde Park roadway leading to the Marble Arch. The screen, built in 1826, is adorned with reliefs copied from those of the frieze of the Parthenon.

60. THE SERPENTINE, HYDE PARK. This long, artificial sheet of water, created by Queen Caroline, wife of George II, is the Londoner's own 'lido' where, in the heat of summer, he may row a boat, bathe, or feed the swans at the water's edge.

61. IN HYDE PARK. London has many lovely parks and gardens, but in none is it more fortunate than in the great open space of Hyde Park. There are upwards of 400 acres of it—which explains why this might be a scene deep in the countryside, a hundred miles from London.

62. GROSVENOR SQUARE. The character of this famous Georgian square in Mayfair has greatly changed in recent years. It was almost completely transformed in 1948 when the statue of President Roosevelt was set up facing an open space of green lawns.

63. REGENT STREET. The massive buildings of one of the world's finest shopping centres, sweeping from Piccadilly Circus to Oxford Street, are a twentieth-century replacement of John Nash's original Regent Street, laid out between 1813 and 1820.

64. BROADCASTING HOUSE, PORTLAND PLACE.　The striking headquarters of the B.B.C. occupies an island site at the northern end of Regent Street. Above the entrance is Eric Gill's sculpture of Prospero and his 'brave spirit' Ariel.

65. THE LAKE IN REGENT'S PARK.   This exquisite park—the home of the Zoo and London's Open Air Theatre—is less than a mile north of Oxford Circus. It was laid out early in the nineteenth century for the Prince Regent by John Nash.

66. KENWOOD, HAMPSTEAD. Left to the nation in 1927 by Lord Iveagh, Kenwood House preserves, on the edge of Hampstead Heath, a fine example of an eighteenth-century country house, with a notable collection of pictures, in a splendid landscape of the period.

67. CHURCH ROW, HAMPSTEAD. The suburb of Hampstead on its steep hill to the north of London retains much of the grace and beauty of its past as a village and fashionable spa. Church Row, with its dignified Georgian houses, is at the heart of 'village' Hampstead.

68. THE ROYAL ALBERT HALL. The view from Kensington Road of London's largest hall in which there is room for up to 10,000 people to hear a concert, watch a prize-fight, or attend a political meeting. It was begun in 1876 as a memorial to the Prince Consort.

69. IN WILTON CRESCENT, WESTMINSTER. A view typical of the quiet and still elegant quarter between Knightsbridge and Buckingham Palace Road, called Belgravia. The church in the background is St Paul's, Knightsbridge, built in the middle of the nineteenth century.

70. IN ROTTEN ROW. This well-known ride stretches for more than a mile from Hyde Park Corner through Hyde Park. The name is said to be a corruption of 'route du roi'—the King's Way.

71. KENSINGTON GARDENS. The gardens adjoin Hyde Park, but preserve their identity to the point of using the name 'Long Water' to describe their stretch of the Serpentine. Overlooking this water is Sir George Frampton's well-loved statue of Peter Pan.

72. WILTON PLACE, BELGRAVIA. The squares and streets of this area are among the best examples of early nineteenth-century building left to London. They date from about 1820–30 on a site transformed by a great builder of the time, Thomas Cubitt.

73. CANNING PLACE, KENSINGTON. The view of Kensington Gate from Canning Place, whose name recalls the fact that the statesman George Canning lived nearby in the second decade of the nineteenth century.

74. IN KENSINGTON GATE. The imposing houses of this small square off the Gloucester Road were built in 1850, thus demonstrating that not all Victorian building was lacking in elegance and architectural good manners.

75. KYNANCE MEWS, KENSINGTON. London's many picturesque mews are survivals from the days of the horse. The stables now either house motor-cars or have been converted into flats. The towers in the background of this photograph are of the Imperial Institute.

76. CHEYNE WALK, CHELSEA. One of the loveliest rows of houses in London. Cheyne Walk faces the Thames and has been the home of many famous writers and artists, among them George Eliot, Rossetti, and Thomas Carlyle.

77. THE ROYAL HOSPITAL, CHELSEA.   The portico and cupola of the main building of the home in London of the scarlet-coated veterans of Britain's armies. It was founded in 1682 by Charles II, and designed (though since altered and enlarged) by Sir Christopher Wren.

78. IN GLEBE PLACE, CHELSEA.   Not many generations have passed since Chelsea was one of London's 'villages', and here and there the passer-by may still come across corners such as this, which might belong to the high street of a village deep in the country.

79. LOTS ROAD POWER STATION, CHELSEA.   Chelsea's river front is not all a stretch gracious with trees and dignified houses.
The chimneys (275 feet high) of its huge power station make an impressive monument of the Age of Electricity.

89. THE COURTYARD OF FULHAM PALACE. The palace on the north bank of the Thames has been for hundreds of years the home of the Bishops of London. The courtyard, with its diamond pattern of black bricks on red, was built in the early years of the reign of Henry VIII.

81. LAMBETH PALACE. The view across the Thames of the Tudor gatehouse (and beyond it, the old church of St Mary's) of the palace that has for seven hundred years been the residence in London of the Archbishops of Canterbury.

82. CHISWICK HOUSE. The flights of steps leading to the portico of the famous Palladian retreat built on Thames-side by Lord Burlington between 1727 and 1736. The park which surrounds it is the noblest of Chiswick's open spaces.

83. LOWER MALL, HAMMERSMITH. The Mall is certainly the most delightful part of Hammersmith—most westerly of London's boroughs. Its balconied Georgian houses are legacies of a time when this was a summer retreat for fashionable Londoners.

84. IN KEW GARDENS. These glorious gardens on the south bank of the Thames are, at any time of the year, one of the 'sights of London'—though strictly speaking beyond London's boundaries. Full of rare shrubs and trees, they are the headquarters of the Royal Botanic Society.

85. STRAND-ON-THE-GREEN, CHISWICK. Strand-on-the-Green, immediately east of Kew Bridge, was once a Thames-side village. This stretch of its water-front owes much of its charm, however, to the grace of its Georgian houses.

86. 'THE LONDON APPRENTICE', ISLEWORTH. Barges still dock at Isleworth water-front near this famous old inn, as they have been doing for hundreds of years. The name recalls the days when City apprentices rowed up to this place on high days and holidays.

87. RICHMOND BRIDGE, SURREY.   The bridge has been widened since James Paine designed it in 1777; but it remains unspoiled, like Richmond itself whose views of the Thames are unsurpassed in variety and grandeur by those of any other reach of the river.

88. HAMPTON COURT PALACE. The view from Sir Edwin Lutyens's bridge over the Thames of the great royal palace begun by Cardinal Wolsey and 'presented' by him to Henry VIII. Besides much splendid Tudor work, it displays some of the best work of Wren.

THE SECOND COUNTRY LIFE

PICTURE BOOK OF LONDON

THE HOUSES OF PARLIAMENT AND WESTMINSTER BRIDGE, FROM LAMBETH BRIDGE

THE SECOND COUNTRY LIFE

PICTURE BOOK
OF LONDON

PHOTOGRAPHS BY

G. F. ALLEN

WITH AN INTRODUCTION BY

RAYMOND BIRT

COUNTRY LIFE LIMITED

2-10 TAVISTOCK STREET, COVENT GARDEN

LONDON WC 2

First published in 1953
by Country Life Limited
Tavistock Street London WC2
Process engraving by
The Sun Engraving Co Ltd London
Printed in Great Britain by
Balding & Mansell Ltd
London and Wisbech
Fourth Impression 1961

INTRODUCTION

LONDON defies definition. It is the capital of Great Britain and principal city of the Commonwealth. It is the largest city in the world. It houses more people than any city now or in history. It is a county. It is a metropolis whose government is divided among twenty-seven boroughs and two cities, one of which, the City of London, is an independent enclave within the whole, having its own police and its own centuries-old form of administration. It is a 'Great Wen', 'the greatest wonder the world can show to the astonished spirit', 'of all places in the country least typically English', and it is (or was to the poet Dunbar four hundred and fifty years ago) 'the flower of Cities all'. London is all these things, and more, for it is so vast, so various that it is most things to all men. They have loved it and cursed it, longed for it in exile and wished themselves away having gained it, fled from it and journeyed to it from the world over, and have, in their millions, quietly endured it. 'London', to quote again from Dunbar, 'thou art of townes *A per se*': or, less elegantly, 'there's nothing like London'.

We are already back where we began. To define the qualities that make London unique is as impossible as it is to define London itself. For London is perpetually in tumultuous flux. Changeless, it continuously grows and renews itself. Like a river, Time drops its silt over London, leaving in each age its characteristic deposit (and from time to time imprinting deep upon it the scars of calamity). Yet it is a deposit not neatly layered, waiting for a distant spade to uncover, as from the mounds of the dead cities of the youth of the world of men, successive empires lying in dust one above the other; but one capricious, unplanned — disorderly, if you will, except that it is the disorder of that kind of vigorous and untrammelled growth by which a tree shapes towards the light and defers to wind and weather.

And are we not approaching one (perhaps two) of the reasons why 'there's nothing like London'? It may seem bold to use the word 'untrammelled' at a time when 'planning' is gospel and the planners themselves multifold and multiloquious. As to that, the river of Time alone can tell. So far, London has resisted nearly all attempts to prune or plan its exuberant growing. In doing so, it has done no more than reflect, after its fashion, the nature of a people notoriously touchy about dictation of any sort from above, and tolerant to a fault of the whims and eccentricities of their neighbours of whatever degree. In such a climate of opinion, like Topsy, London 'growed'. It was, and still is, as simple as that.

The result is what gives London if not uniqueness then certainly a particularity among capital cities. London is 'as you like it', or rather as its citizens and builders have liked it. Its glory (and the fun of it) is its inconsequence. The face it shows is venerable: one which has lived through it all: danger, romance, frolics, passion of every sort, endeavour, disaster, sobriety — the whole catalogue of sins and virtues, and the sheer accidents of time and change. It is there for all to see, warts and carbuncles and scars scattered among the nobler and happier lines that virtue has drawn where it

will. So that you may stand, for example (as do two pages of this book at plates 18 and 19) where Aldwych meets the Strand, and see as much matter for reflection as would serve a moralist for a bundle of sermons, a satirist with a year's grace of a sense of his self-importance, and a social historian with heaven-knows-how-much excuse for solemn generalities. Here is St Clement Danes ('"oranges and lemons", said the bells of St Clement's'), possibly the site of a church frequented by those Danish kings of England who preceded the Normans, and certainly, after its re-building late in the seventeenth century, Dr Johnson's place of worship, its body destroyed by German fire-bombs early in the last war. Beyond it, the fantastical towers, spires and gables of the Law Courts, a gothicised version of the Scottish baronial style that we owe to the romanticism of the Victorian age. And beyond that the villainously ugly Griffin which stands on its pedestal in the middle of the road guarding the entrance to Fleet Street, and whose horror is mitigated only by its reminder that here stood Temple Bar (now exiled in rural Hertfordshire), the western gate of the City of London, and still the scene today, whenever the sovereign rides by, of medieval pomp and magnificence as the Lord Mayor and Aldermen of the City come out in loyal independence to bar the way, and in loyalty pure to bid Her Majesty welcome. Turn round, and the statue of Gladstone (at his feet four figures symbolic of Aspiration, Education, Brotherhood and Courage) faces the Strand. Appropriately, he gazes Westminster-wards, and not at the massive twentieth-century Australia House, on whose façade (French eighteenth-century above Grecian columns) the vast horses of Phoebus, and the Goddess herself, are the merest incidents. (Every stone of this building is quarried from Australian earth.) And behind the statue is a small relic as significant and as poignant as any: an imperishable trough erected in the last century by the Drinking Fountain and Cattle Trough Association; a memorial at once to the Englishman's love of animals (particularly if they are horses), the amplitude of Victorian philanthropy, and the passing of the long age of the horse in favour of the stink and growl of the internal combustion engine.

There's richness! In this one brief glimpse of London, what journeys in time and space the imagination has achieved. What a multiplicity of memories and response have been evoked. What a variety of emotions have been stirred. It is, after all, understandable that London can often disappoint the visitor eager to be impressed. In-consequence is its genius, and for its interpretation patience is the first need and sympathetic attention the second. But the rewards for both are very great.

For my part, it is for the response that it evokes that I value a book such as this. True, the photographs are admirable in themselves. Many of them are of great beauty, and some, through the skill of their maker, have increased my understanding of the character of London by revealing glimpses of it I had not noticed before. But the enduring pleasure is that of wandering at leisure in London's splendid profusion. I am not arguing that books are a substitute for the real thing. We must go to London, even if, like the pussy-cat who set out to see the Queen, the place is too overpowering for more than the enjoyments familiar to our own fireside. For London crowds are relentless, its traffic a terror, and its streets as unquiet as a river in spate. There is little place or opportunity here for the reflective man, who may best evoke the spirit of London by remembering it in tranquility.

These pages are an invitation to explore, as it might be by celestial omnibus. To the City itself, where William the Norman's Tower is neighbour to Roman walls, and where serious men of affairs, in robes and gowns, piously remember their predecessors of more than eight hundred years by walking with brooms and nosegays through streets no longer running with filth and offensive to a delicate nose. Or where markets for fish and for game inconveniently persist in the shadow of great commercial palaces because they were there by prior right of possession. Or where Wren's glorious towers and spires still ennoble the skyline in despite of all the destroyers, not least among them the twentieth-century airplane. Here is Tudor London in the uniform of the Yeomen of the Guard, and in the friendly informality of the gateway of St James's Palace, just off Piccadilly. Here are the memories of Elizabethan England on Shakespeare's Bankside where a tavern or two and a few street names are potent guardians, among cranes and warehouses, of an unforgettable past. Here, in Whitehall, Charles Stuart walked to his death through a window of the Banqueting House, built for his royal father by Inigo Jones. And there is the Hospital built at the command of the second Charles to house the veterans of England's wars. It is all here: the harmony of Queen Anne building, Georgian elegance, Victorian muddle and grandeur, Edwardian opulence, and . . . but let us beware of finding epithets for ourselves. Others will later on most certainly do it for us when they stand (for example) on the Victoria Embankment and make their judgment on Waterloo Bridge and the Festival Hall on South Bank. As they, and what they have made of London, will also be judged in turn.

For London lives and grows: tenacious of all its past, tolerant and patient of the fret of its present, and utterly secure in its continuance and its power to move the imagination and affection of those who are, for a little while, its inheritors.

1953   RAYMOND BIRT

LIST OF PLATES

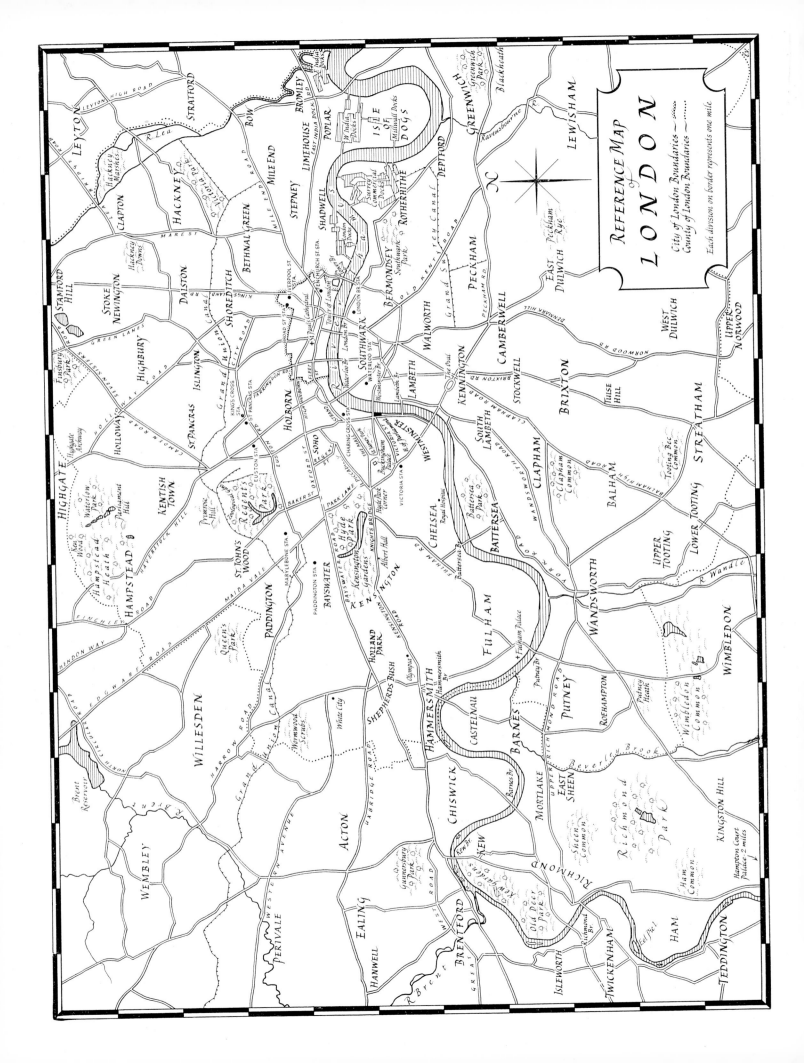

PARLIAMENT SQUARE. The towers of Westminster Abbey, seen across this famous square, which was redesigned in 1951. In the foreground, the statue of Benjamin Disraeli, Earl of Beaconsfield.

2. NELSON'S COLUMN, TRAFALGAR SQUARE. The giant figure of Nelson, 184 feet above the ground, was placed on its column in November, 1843. The square itself was laid out as a national war memorial between 1829 and 1841.

. **THE FOUNTAINS OF TRAFALGAR SQUARE.** There are very few visitors to London who do not come here to feed the pigeons, inspect Landseer's bronze lions, and listen to the fountains. These last are post-war additions to the amenities of the square.

4. THE ADMIRALTY ARCH, FROM THE MALL. The Arch closes the great avenue of the Mall where it leads into Trafalgar Square. It was built in 1910 as part of the national memorial to Queen Victoria. In the foreground is the statue of Captain Cook.

5. WHITEHALL, SOUTH FROM THE STATUE OF THE DUKE OF CAMBRIDGE. On the left is the Banqueting House, built for James I by Inigo Jones. Through one of its windows, Charles I walked to his execution on January 30, 1649.

6. BUCKINGHAM PALACE, FROM THE VICTORIA MEMORIAL. The Royal Standard flying at the flagstaff tells London that the Queen is in residence. The crowd collects by the railings and around the Victoria Memorial to watch the changing of the guard.

. **LIFE GUARDS ON CONSTITUTION HILL.**   On its way to the Horse Guards, the detachment passes the triumphal arch designed
by Decimus Burton in 1828, and crowned, a hundred years later, by Adrian Jones's figure of Peace alighting on the chariot of war.

8. GUARD DUTY AT BUCKINGHAM PALACE. A detachment of the Guards marches out from Wellington Barracks, in Birdcage Walk, for its turn of guard-mounting at Buckingham Palace.

9. A CORNER OF ST JAMES'S PARK.   Beyond the trees that border the lake rises the campanile (273 feet high) of Westminster Cathedral, begun in 1892 to the design of J. F. Bentley.

10. TULIP TIME IN HYDE PARK. Like all the great parks of London, Hyde Park was once a royal hunting and pleasure ground. But it has been open to the public for more than 300 years—the best-known and best-loved of all London's open spaces.

11. CARLTON HOUSE TERRACE. This distinguished group of buildings faces the Mall and St James's Park. It was built in 1831, and, after housing Prime Ministers, statesmen, ambassadors, and many famous men, now largely provides space for Government offices.

12. IN BELGRAVE SQUARE. This famous square, the heart of once-aristocratic and still fashionable Belgravia, was built in 1825 by Thomas Cubitt, one of the great contractors and builders of the early nineteenth century.

13. THE ATHENÆUM, PALL MALL. The architect of this most distinguished of London's clubs, completed in 1830, was Decimus Burton. Above the portico stands a gilded figure of Pallas Athene. The statue on the right is that of Florence Nightingale.

14. ST JAMES'S STREET, EARLY MORNING. This well-known West End street is one of the links between Piccadilly and Pall Mall. At its southern end is the gateway of St James's Palace, built more than four hundred years ago by Henry VIII.

15. BURLINGTON ARCADE, PICCADILLY. The arcade lies off Piccadilly to the west of Burlington House, home of the Royal Academy, the Royal Society, and other learned societies. It is a famous and elegant shopping centre dating from 1818.

16. NEW COURT, MIDDLE TEMPLE. The Temple, which lies between Fleet Street and the Thames, has been the home of the lawyers of the Inner and Middle Temples since the fourteenth century. New Court was the last of the courts to be added—in 1676.

MERSET HOUSE, FROM THE STRAND.   Somerset House, built on the site of a royal palace of the same name, was designed by Sir William Chambers and begun in 1776. It now houses the offices of the Inland Revenue and the Registrar General.

18. ST CLEMENT DANES AND THE LAW COURTS IN THE STRAND. The island church is known all over the world, for its bells are those which said 'oranges and lemons' in the nursery rhyme. The body of the church was destroyed by bombs in 1940.

AT THE JUNCTION OF THE ALDWYCH AND THE STRAND. The view is to the west along the Strand. Here Hamo Thornycroft's bronze statue of W. E. Gladstone faces the massive façade of Australia House, opened by King George V in 1918.

20. EVENING IN THE CITY. Against the western sky are the silhouettes of the skeleton roof of Cannon Street station, St Paul Cathedral, the tower and steeple of St Magnus the Martyr, and the Monument.

SKYLINE OF THE CITY OF LONDON. In the foreground are the buildings of the Temple. Against the sky the dominant landmarks are the Old Bailey (left), the magnificent spire of Wren's church of St Bride, and St Paul's Cathedral.

22. WITHIN ST PAUL'S CATHEDRAL. The view from the choir stalls of the nave and south aisle. The carving of the stalls a organ case is by Grinling Gibbons; below the dome can be seen one of the mosaics which were added in the nineteenth century.

MESSENGERS OF THE BANK OF ENGLAND. They stand, in their glossy top-hats and tail-coats, in the great portico of the Royal Exchange. In the background is the main portico of Sir Herbert Baker's new Bank of England building, completed in 1940.

24. THE MANSION HOUSE. The official home of the Lord Mayor of London overlooks the busiest traffic crossing in the City. Th
imposing building was designed by George Dance the Elder, and erected between 1738 and 1752.

5. **THE CITY OF LONDON'S GUILDHALL.**   The front of Guildhall was the work of George Dance the Younger in 1789. The hall itself dates back at least to the fifteenth century. It was severely damaged by the Great Fire of 1666 and by fire-bombs in 1940.

26. FISH-PORTERS OF BILLINGSGATE MARKET. Ships have called at Billingsgate since Roman times, though it was not until the end of the seventeenth century that it became primarily a market for fish. Beyond is the tower and lantern of St Magnus the Martyr

7. LEADENHALL MARKET. There has been a market here in the heart of the City, four hundred yards from the Bank of England, since 1357. It still deals in poultry and game, as it did then.

28. PROCESSION OF THE VINTNERS' COMPANY.   Annually in July members of this ancient city company walk from their Hall to the church of St James Garlickhithe for a thanksgiving service. The custom dates from as far back as 1205.

79. THE COLLEGE OF ARMS, QUEEN VICTORIA STREET. This pleasant brick building, dating from after the Great Fire, is the headquarters of the officers of the college—the heralds—whose splendid uniforms are a feature of some of the great occasions of state.

30. THE TOWER OF LONDON, FROM SOUTH BANK. The turreted and massive White Tower is the oldest part of the fortres
It was begun in the reign of William the Conqueror on a site that the Roman legionaries had used before him.

31. TOWER BRIDGE, FROM HAYS WHARF. The bridge was built between 1886 and 1894. The high footway between the two towers has been closed for over forty years; but the arms of the road-bridge are lifted daily to let river traffic pass.

32. WITHIN THE TOWER OF LONDON. Beyond the sentry and the rays of the early morning sun is the Wakefield Tower, built in the reign of Edward I (1239-1307). Here in 1471 Henry VI was put to death.

IE BYWARD TOWER, TOWER OF LONDON. Now used by the Yeomen Warders, the Byward Tower was formerly the
ce at which the pass-word was given by visitors to the castle. Its door is still locked every night during the Ceremony of the Keys.

34. THE COURT OF STAPLE INN, HOLBORN.   Once one of the Inns of Court (in which Mr Grewgious of Dickens's
had his lodgings), Staple Inn is now a quiet sanctuary off Holborn, where City workers may enjoy their midday br

NEW SQUARE, LINCOLN'S INN. Lincoln's Inn has been the home of lawyers and barristers since the fourteenth century.
New Square—damaged during the second World War—dates from the seventeenth century.

36. RUPERT COURT, SOHO. Soho, between Shaftesbury Avenue and Oxford Street, is unlike any other part of London. This is the quarter of foreigners, restaurants, cafés, and film companies' offices—a combination that gives Soho its slightly exotic quality.

7. IN THE FLORAL HALL, COVENT GARDEN. Covent Garden is London's greatest market for fruit, vegetables and flowers, which have been sold on this site since early in the seventeenth century.

38. DOWNRIVER FROM THE VICTORIA EMBANKMENT. Six bridges cross this stretch of the Thames: Blackfriars and its railway bridge, Southwark, Cannon Street railway bridge, London Bridge, and Tower Bridge.

9. UPRIVER FROM THE VICTORIA EMBANKMENT. The two bridges are the Waterloo (1937-44) and the Charing Cross railway bridge. In the foreground is Scott's ship, the *Discovery*. To the left is the Clock Tower of the Houses of Parliament.

40. IN BOROUGH MARKET, SOUTHWARK. A busy market for vegetables and fruit fills the streets around Southwark Cathedral, whose tower dates from about 1520. The market has been established here since the days of Edward VI.

. THE ANCHOR TAVERN ON BANKSIDE.   A van rattles over the streets of Bankside, in Tudor times a pleasure garden where bulls were baited and Shakespeare's plays presented at the 'Globe'. There was an Anchor tavern on this site in Shakespeare's day.

42. THE GEORGE INN, SOUTHWARK. The George is the last of the galleried inns of London, and the building dates from 167
The inn-yard is annually the scene of productions of an Elizabethan play and a scene from one of Dickens's novels.

WAREHOUSES, BANKSIDE. The river front between Southwark and London Bridge is now claimed by tall warehouses, most of them of nineteenth-century building. In the background is the shadowy outline of the tower of Southwark Cathedral.

44. THE ROYAL FESTIVAL HALL. The most recent of the great public buildings of London was built on the Festival of Brita
site in 1951. It has established itself as one of the finest halls for music-making in the world.

5. THE THAMES FROM COUNTY HALL.   From the terrace of County Hall, headquarters of the London County Council, the view down river is of great blocks of office buildings and hotels, dominated by the massive clock-tower of Shell-Mex House.

46. THE ROYAL HOSPITAL, CHELSEA.   This home for old soldiers was founded by Charles II, and designed by Sir Christophe
Wren. The pensioners' scarlet and blue uniforms are a familiar part of the London scene.

7. RIVERSIDE LIGHTS OF BATTERSEA PARK. Beyond the lights of the Pleasure Gardens, laid out for the Festival of Britain in 1951, stands one of the least pleasing of Thames road-bridges—the Albert Bridge, built in 1873.

48. THE ORANGERY, KENSINGTON PALACE.   This is one of the most beautiful of Sir Christopher Wren's buildings. He designe
it in red brick for Queen Anne in 1704.

49. OLD KENSINGTON. These cottages near Kensington Palace are lovely survivals of the days when Sir Christopher Wren and William Kent were building and embellishing the Palace for Queen Anne and George I.

50. CHURCH WALK, KENSINGTON. Behind Kensington High Street and its great stores lies this little street of one-man shops—
a centre typical of the hundreds of small 'neighbourhoods' that make up residential London.

51. CONVERSATION PIECE, KENSINGTON. The scene is eloquent of the character of the Royal Borough—of that part of it, at least, which lies around Church Row, where life (and architecture) are decorous, in good taste, and firmly linked to past glories.

52. CHURCHES OF KENSINGTON. On the left, Holy Trinity, Brompton's parish church. On the right, the Brompton Oratory, built in the Renaissance style in the 1880s, of which Cardinal Newman was one of the founders.

53. THE LONG WATER, KENSINGTON GARDENS. The Long Water is in fact part of the Serpentine. Here, where the fountains play near the Marlborough Gate, is one of the most enchanting parts of a lovely corner of London.

54. THE REGENCY TERRACES, REGENT'S PARK. These glorious terraces, designed by John Nash and Decimus Burton, face the park on the east and west. They were severely damaged during the second World War, but have been for the most part restored.

55. IN SUSSEX PLACE, REGENT'S PARK.   Houses which typify the elegance of the Regency buildings around this lovely park. Its layout was begun in 1812, and the park was first opened to the public in 1838.

56. AUTUMN IN REGENT'S PARK. A scene in Broad Walk, a tree-lined avenue that runs for about a mile across the park, which includes within its boundaries the Open Air Theatre and the Zoo.

CANAL SCENE, PADDINGTON. London has few canals, but those it has are not only useful but also pictorially rewarding. This is a view of the Grand Junction which begins at Paddington and links London by water to the Midlands and the North.

58. HOLLY BUSH HILL, HAMPSTEAD. Hampstead is built on one of the highest hills of London, and is full of pleasant hou
many of them, now and in the past, the homes of distinguished or famous men. George Romney's studio still stands on Holly Bush

THE SHEPHERD ON THE LONDON HILLS.   A scene in Ken Wood, the splendid stretch of parkland in Highgate which was handed over to Londoners in 1924.

60. ON CHISWICK MALL. The Mall is a delightful riverside walk with a number of charming old houses. In the churchyard of Nicholas, whose tower dates from the fifteenth century, William Hogarth lies buried.

THE THAMES AT RICHMOND. Richmond, with its glorious park and river scenery and its handsome houses, is just beyond the borders of the County of London; but few Londoners do not feel that Richmond is as much 'theirs' as Hyde Park and the Serpentine.

62. THE GREAT GATEHOUSE, HAMPTON COURT PALACE. Wolsey's palace of rose-red brick is probably the most love
as it is certainly one of the most popular, attractions around London. It was a favourite royal home until the death, in 1760, of George

8. THE VILLAGE POND, MILL HILL. Mill Hill lies to the north-west of Hampstead and belongs to Middlesex, not to London. It retains some of its village character, though on either side the suburbs of London have swallowed up the hills and green fields.

64. THE TATE GALLERY, MILLBANK. Built between 1893 and 1897 on the north bank of the Thames between Lambeth and Vauxhall bridges, the Tate Gallery houses collections of the work of British artists, and of modern paintings chiefly of the French school.

65. ST PAUL'S CHURCH, SHADWELL. Shadwell is a Thames-side parish in London's dockland. The church, which in its present form was built in 1821, is seen across the water of Shadwell Basin.

66. THE GEFFRYE MUSEUM, SHOREDITCH. This was once a group of almshouses built in 1715 under the will of Sir Robert Geffrye, a Lord Mayor of London. It was opened as a museum of furniture and house furnishings in 1914.

67. IN DULWICH VILLAGE, CAMBERWELL. There is nothing quite like Dulwich in all London. Four miles south of the City and surrounded by thickly populated suburbs, the old village survives virtually untouched by marks of the last hundred years.

68. GEORGIAN HOUSES ON BLACKHEATH. This common has seen many great events in English history—among them the musters of the Kentish rebels of Wat Tyler and Jack Cade, and the meeting between the citizens of London and Henry V after Agincourt.

69. THE PARAGON, BLACKHEATH. This beautiful crescent of houses at the south-east corner of the Heath was built about 1800. It was severely damaged by German bombs during the second World War but has now been restored.

70. IN THE ROYAL DOCKS. The group of docks composed of the Royal Victoria, the Royal Albert and the King George V is the largest of its kind in the world, having a water area of 246 acres. The King George V (in which this photograph was taken) was opened in 1921.

71. ROYAL NAVAL COLLEGE, GREENWICH. The view is towards the river from Observatory Hill. In the foreground, the beautiful Queen's House, designed by Inigo Jones, and completed in 1635. It is now part of the National Maritime Museum.

72. THE THAMES AT DEPTFORD. High tide, and a winter's sun going down before its time behind the clouds and smoke above London's dockland.

THE THIRD COUNTRY LIFE

PICTURE BOOK OF LONDON

BUCKINGHAM PALACE SEEN FROM ST JAMES'S PARK IN SPRINGTIME

THE THIRD COUNTRY LIFE

PICTURE BOOK

OF LONDON

PHOTOGRAPHS BY

G. F. ALLEN

COUNTRY LIFE LIMITED LONDON

First published in 1956
by Country Life Limited
Tavistock Street London W.C.2
Printed in Great Britain by
Balding & Mansell Ltd
London and Wisbech

LIST OF PLATES

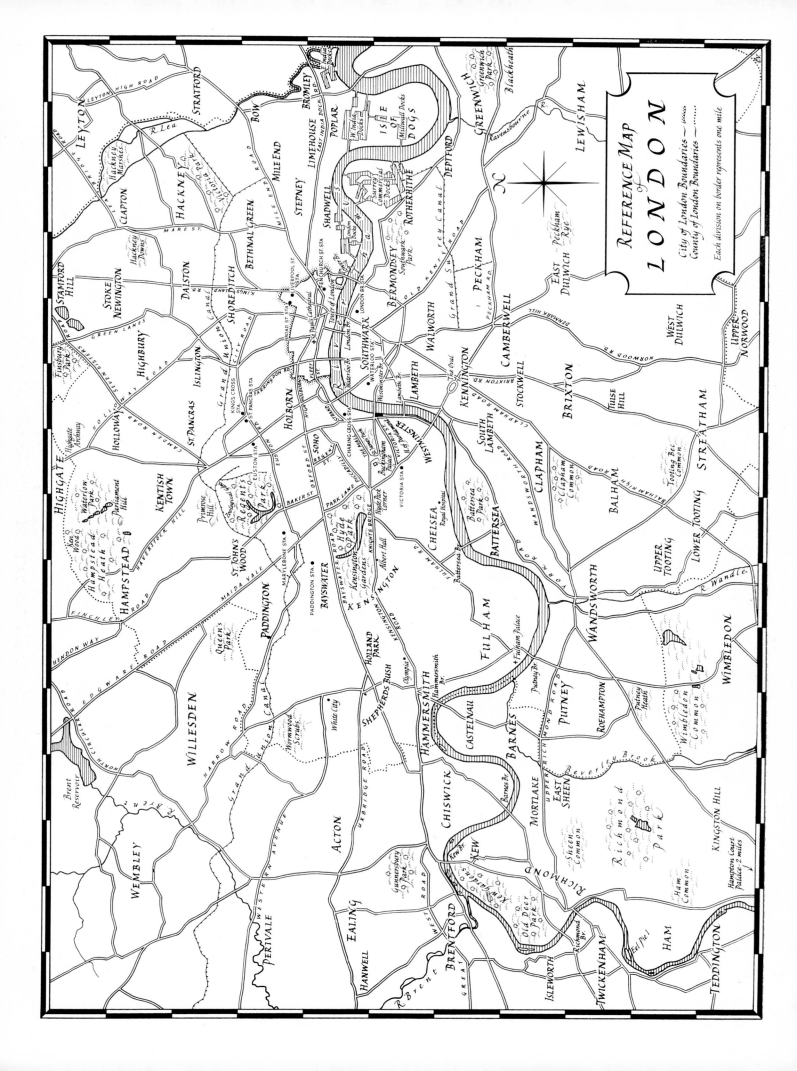

1. FOUR CITY BRIDGES CROSS THE THAMES. A panoramic view showing Southwark Bridge in the foreground, then Cannon Street railway bridge, London Bridge and, in the distance, Tower Bridge.

2. ST JAMES'S PALACE BY FLOODLIGHT. Reflections on one of the rain-washed courtyards of this famous royal residence where
Charles I spent the last nights before his execution.

3. THE CHANGING OF THE GUARD. After the ceremony, the pipers of the Scots Guards are proceeding down the Mall to St James's Palace, with the Victoria Memorial and Buckingham Palace in the background.

4. CARLTON HOUSE TERRACE FLOODLIT. This graceful row of buildings on the north side of the Mall was built in 1831 on the
site of what used to be the garden of Carlton House.

5. THE NATIONAL GALLERY. The classical pattern of Carlton House Terrace is continued in the National Gallery, in Trafalgar Square, for the columns of the portico were once those of Carlton House.

6. CHRISTMAS EVE IN TRAFALGAR SQUARE. The sparkling Christmas Tree—an annual gift from the people of Norway—and the floodlit fountains give a fairy-tale touch to London's most celebrated square.

7. BIG BEN FROM TRAFALGAR SQUARE. A telephoto lens was used for this view down Whitehall from the portico of the National Gallery, with the statues of Charles I and Earl Haig in the centre.

8. TROOPING THE COLOUR. Preceded by the massed bands, Her Majesty The Queen leads the Guards on the return to Buckingham Palace at the end of the annual ceremony on Horse Guards Parade.

9. NUMBER TEN DOWNING STREET. A lamp hangs over the door of the rather dreary-looking official residence of the Prime Minister, off Whitehall, and policemen are always on guard.

10. WESTMINSTER SCHOOL. Around Little Dean's Yard are grouped the main buildings of London's most famous public school, among whose scholars were Ben Jonson, Dryden, Christopher Wren and Warren Hastings.

1. KING HENRY VII'S CHAPEL, WESTMINSTER ABBEY. Begun in 1502, this is the most modern of the great buildings of the Abbey. The banners are those of the Knights of the Bath.

12. SUMMER EVENING IN ST JAMES'S PARK. Looking across the tranquil water of the lake in the famous park where many Prime Ministers have strolled and many lovers have sat.

13. WESTMINSTER PANORAMA. The view from the Clock Tower of the Houses of Parliament. Beyond Parliament Square is the Middlesex Guildhall and the Central Hall, Westminster, where the first United Nations Assembly met in 1946.

14. THE HOUSE OF LORDS. Looking down on the Chamber from the Peeresses' Gallery one sees the Queen's magnificent Throne and the curiously-shaped Woolsack on which the Lord Chancellor sits.

15. THE HOUSE OF COMMONS. The Speaker's Chair and the Government Benches in the Chamber that has arisen on the site of the old one destroyed by bombing in the Second World War.

16. NEW SCOTLAND YARD. On the Victoria Embankment, beyond the busy river, stands the headquarters of the Metropolitan Police, a building that has made the words 'Scotland Yard' famous throughout the world.

17. COUNTY HALL, WESTMINSTER. Floodlighting gives a curiously Oriental effect to this photograph of the headquarters of the London County Council on the South Bank of the Thames.

18. ROUGH WATER ON THE THAMES. In this unusual photograph a party of sea-cadets are sailing their little craft past their training-ship, *Discovery*, in which Captain Scott sailed to the Antarctic.

19. THE VICTORIA EMBANKMENT. The tree-lined Embankment with *Discovery*, *Wellington* and *Chrysanthemum* the foreground. The tall spire in the centre is that of St Bride's, Fleet Street.

20. IN THE HEART OF CLUBLAND. Several of London's celebrated social clubs are situated in St James's Street, including Boodle's (designed by Robert Adam and seen here), White's and Brooks's.

21. THE DUKE OF YORK'S STATUE. This photograph taken from Waterloo Place, at the foot of Lower Regent Street, gives an unusual view of the statue, with the towers of Westminster in the background.

22. A PAVEMENT ARTIST. His pictures will never be exhibited at the Royal Academy, but the Pavement Artist is a familiar sight in London and his work is often of a surprisingly high standard.

23. THE ROYAL ACADEMY. To give it its full title, 'The Royal Academy of Arts in London, for the Purpose of Cultivating and Improving the Arts of Painting, Sculpture and Architecture' was founded in 1768.

24. HYDE PARK CORNER. On the south side of Hyde Park stands the triple-arched gateway, erected in 1828 from Decimus Burton's designs; here it is seen from the park across Rotten Row.

25. THE MARBLE ARCH. At the other end of the park from Hyde Park Corner is the Marble Arch. Designed in 1827 by John Nash, it formed the entrance to Buckingham Palace until 1851.

26. ST GEORGE'S, HANOVER SQUARE. Built between 1712–25, this church has been since the early nineteenth century the scene of many fashionable weddings, including that of Theodore Roosevelt, later President of the United States.

27. BROADCASTING HOUSE, PORTLAND PLACE. The rounded outlines of the headquarters of the B.B.C. are in keeping with those of the church of All Souls, Langham Place, in the foreground.

C

28. TWO GREAT ACTORS. Two of the most famous names in the theatrical world are linked in this picture in which the statue of Sir Henry Irving overlooks the Garrick Theatre in Charing Cross Road.

29. THE THEATRE ROYAL, HAYMARKET. One of London's oldest theatres—it was rebuilt in 1821—seen from near John Bacon's statue of William III in St James's Square.

30. ST PAUL'S, COVENT GARDEN. The present building is a copy of the original church which was destroyed by fire in 1795 and which its designer, Inigo Jones, once called 'the finest barn in Europe'.

31. COVENT GARDEN MARKET. When St Paul's Church was first built in 1631, its piazza was used by sellers of fruit and vegetables ;
the area around it is now one of London's chief—and most congested—markets.

32. BETWEEN FLEET STREET AND THE STRAND. The griffin statue in the middle of the road, opposite the Law Courts, marks the site of the old Temple Bar which divided the Cities of London and Westminster.

33. IN THE MIDDLE TEMPLE. The stairs lead up to Garden Court and in the background is Middle Temple Hall, badly damaged by incendiary bombs in 1941, but restored in 1949.

34. MIDDLE TEMPLE HALL. The equestrian portrait of Charles I, attributed to Van Dyck, and those of other Kings and Queens gaze down on the Hall where *Twelfth Night* was performed in 1602, possibly by Shakespeare's own company.

35. THE HALL OF GRAY'S INN. The magnificent Hall of the Inn—it owes its name to the Lords Grey of Wilton—has now been rebuilt after being practically destroyed by bombing in 1941.

36. ST BARTHOLOMEW THE GREAT, SMITHFIELD. Passing through this thirteenth-century archway, with an early seventeenth-century house-front above it, you come to what is London's oldest church apart from the Tower Chapel.

37. STAPLE INN, HOLBORN. Much restored, this is one of the few remaining half-timbered house-fronts in London. Dr Johnson once lived in this old Inn of Chancery.

38. BEDFORD SQUARE, BLOOMSBURY. Some of the magnificent plane trees in this square which was built between 1775 and 1780 on what was part of the Duke of Bedford's extensive London estate.

39. A COURTYARD OF THE CHARTERHOUSE. This famous home of the 'poor brethren'—it is a corruption of 'Chartreuse' and was formerly a Carthusian priory—is recovering from severe bomb damage sustained in the Second World War.

40. THE HOME OF CHARLES DICKENS. At number forty-eight Doughty Street, in the angle between Theobald's Road and Gray's Inn Road, Dickens lived from March, 1837, to the end of 1839, and wrote *Oliver Twist* and *Nicholas Nickleby*.

41. DR JOHNSON'S HOUSE. Just off Fleet Street, at number seventeen Gough Square, Samuel Johnson lived between 1748 and 1759, labouring in the attic with his assistants on his famous Dictionary.

42. ST PAUL'S FROM KING EDWARD STREET. This unusual glimpse of the Cathedral is obtained from the north, looking across Newgate Street. The statue in silhouette is of Sir Rowland Hill, the postal reformer.

43. QUEEN ANNE'S STATUE AND THE OLD BAILEY. From the site of the statue—a nineteenth-century copy of the original—in front of St Paul's one can see the dome of the Old Bailey, crowned by the statue of Justice with sword and scales.

D

44. THE MONUMENT. Christopher Wren designed both the Monument, which commemorates the Fire of London, and the church of St Magnus the Martyr, the curious tower of which is seen in the foreground.

45. 'THE OLD LADY OF THREADNEEDLE STREET'. Outside the Bank of England stands a statue of the Duke of Wellington—
without hat, boots, saddle or stirrups—made from guns captured from the French.

46. THE APOTHECARIES' HALL, BLACKFRIARS LANE. The original Hall of the Company was destroyed in the Fire of London; its successor, built on the same site, dates from 1670, being restored in 1929.

47. LOMBARD STREET. The hanging signs of the banking and other City business houses remind us of the old proverbial saying 'All Lombard Street to a China orange'.

48. BILLINGSGATE MARKET. Established on the banks of the Thames close to London Bridge in 1699 as a 'free and open fish market',
Billingsgate has been famous for its fish—and its language—ever since.

49. SUNDAY MORNING IN 'PETTICOAT LANE'. Although it is now officially Middlesex Street, everybody calls this famous Whitechapel street-market by its old name 'Petticoat Lane'.

50. THE OLDEST CHAPEL IN LONDON. In the Chapel Royal of St John the Evangelist, within the Tower of London, the Knights of the Bath formerly spent the night before their investiture.

51. CHURCH PARADE ON TOWER GREEN. The Yeoman Warders, in their picturesque Tudor uniforms, are being inspected by the Resident Governor and Major of the Tower of London.

52. TOWER BRIDGE. In this photograph taken from below London Bridge, the twin bascules or drawbridges have been raised to allow the passage of a ship passing down the Thames.

53. LAMBETH WALK. To quote the dance-song, these three residents might be said to be 'doing the Lambeth Walk', eating their fish-and-chips as they pass beneath the signs of public house and pawnbroker.

54. ST SAVIOUR'S WHARF, BERMONDSEY. A typical Thameside Wharf on London's South Bank in the borough of Bermondsey, noted for centuries for its tanneries and leather works, still to be seen—and smelled.

55. TRANQUIL VALE, BLACKHEATH. These old houses in Blackheath, just south of Greenwich Park, stand in what is surely one of the most quaintly-named streets in London.

56. THE PAINTED HALL, GREENWICH. Designed by Wren and with wall paintings by Thornhill, this was the Royal Hospital refectory before the building was taken over by the Royal Naval College.

57. A SAILING SHIP ON THE THAMES. At anchor above the Royal Naval College, Greenwich, is the Italian three-masted training ship, *Amerigo Vespucci*—a type of ship familiar enough centuries ago.

58. THE FLASK INN, HIGHGATE. This ancient inn probably gets its name from the fact that flasks could be obtained there to be filled with water from the Hampstead medicinal wells.

59. GOLDEN YARD, HAMPSTEAD. 'Peach Tree Cottage' is typical of the many quaint houses tucked away in odd corners of this northern part of London, once very much a village.

60. ROMNEY'S HOUSE, HAMPSTEAD. Standing by a little green at the top of Hollybush Hill, and dating from about 1700, is the boarded house which was the painter's last home before he returned to Kendal to die.

61. HAPPY HAMPSTEAD. The phrase 'Like Hampstead Heath on a Bank Holiday' has become part of the language; this is what it looks like with the fair in full swing.

62. A MEWS IN BELGRAVIA. What used to be the stables of houses in Wilton Place, in this once extremely fashionable quarter, are now in themselves delightful little residences, gay with sunblinds and fresh paint.

63. A ROOF GARDEN IN KENSINGTON. There is a tropical air about this roof garden of a well-known store, overlooked by the tall and graceful spire of St Mary Abbots church.

64. THE ROYAL ALBERT HALL. This unusual view of the world-famous concert hall is taken from the back. Built in the Italian Renaissance style in 1867–71, it holds 10,000 people.

65. KENSINGTON PALACE. The Clock Tower overlooking the Jacobean Quadrangle of the palace which was partly built by Wren for William and Mary and partly by Kent for George I. Queen Victoria was born here.

66. CHEYNE WALK, CHELSEA. Many artists and writers have made their home in this street that runs near the river; the plaque states that George Eliot once lived at number four.

67. CHELSEA PENSIONERS. An unself-concious pose by two of the red-coated veterans who live at the Royal Hospital, Chelsea, the home for old soldiers founded by Charles II.

68. STRAND ON THE GREEN. On the edge of the Thames, between Kew Bridge and Chiswick Bridge, stands this row of little early-Georgian houses, very fashionable two hundred years ago.

69. THE PALM HOUSE, KEW GARDENS. One of the sights of the Royal Botanical Gardens, covering 288 acres, is the Palm House designed by Decimus Burton and completed in 1848.

70. THE VIEW FROM RICHMOND HILL. From the Terrace Gardens one gets this superb view of the Thames valley that inspired many artists including Sir Joshua Reynolds and Turner.

71. AN OLD INN AT ROEHAMPTON. To the east of Richmond Park and to the north of Wimbledon Common is Roehampton, from which these young riders can be sure of finding country-like surroundings.

72. HAMPTON COURT PALACE. Although outside the bounds of London, the great palace is easily accessible; here, seen across the pond, is the main facade built by Sir Christopher Wren.

73. WINDSOR CASTLE FROM THE LONG WALK. Again outside London, but easily reached, is the castle begun in the reign of William the Conqueror. The Round Tower on the left is the ancient Keep.

74. WESTMINSTER BY FLOODLIGHT. This fine picture of the floodlit Houses of Parliament, the Big Ben Tower and Westminster Abbey—with the Boadicea statue in silhouette—brings the book to a fitting close.